The Great Kite

Virginia Avniel Spatz

Charnice Milton Community Bookstore
1918 Martin Luther King Jr. Avenue, SE
Washington, DC 20020

The Great Kite
(c) 2019 Virginia Avniel Spatz

ISBN 978-1-7344418-0-2

This publication is offered to encourage reading, imagination, and conversation about books and ideas. We hope that this publication will inspire readers to create and share their own words, artwork, and books.

Instead of professional illustration, this edition includes the author's untrained, raw drawings as part of an encouragement to the reader to fill in their own visions. A new edition, with additional artwork, is planned.

in memory of Bob Rovinsky (8/25/46-10/24/19)
master storyteller,
teacher of Judaism,
and friend to many

and in memory of Charnice Milton (6/19/87 - 5/27/15)
journalist, lover of books,
and supporter of
east of the river, DC

Charnice Milton Community Bookstore
1918 Martin Luther King Jr. Avenue, SE
Washington, DC 20020
weluvbooks.org

The Great Kite is a story...

> ...and some prompts for thinking, writing, and artwork.

Many very young readers
and some of all ages
will want to read
the story by itself.

Story text looks like this.

> Many older readers,
> and some young ones, maybe with a little help,
> will enjoy reading prompts
> and using some
> or all of them
> for their own creations
> while reading this one.
>
> Prompts look like this.

Story starts here.

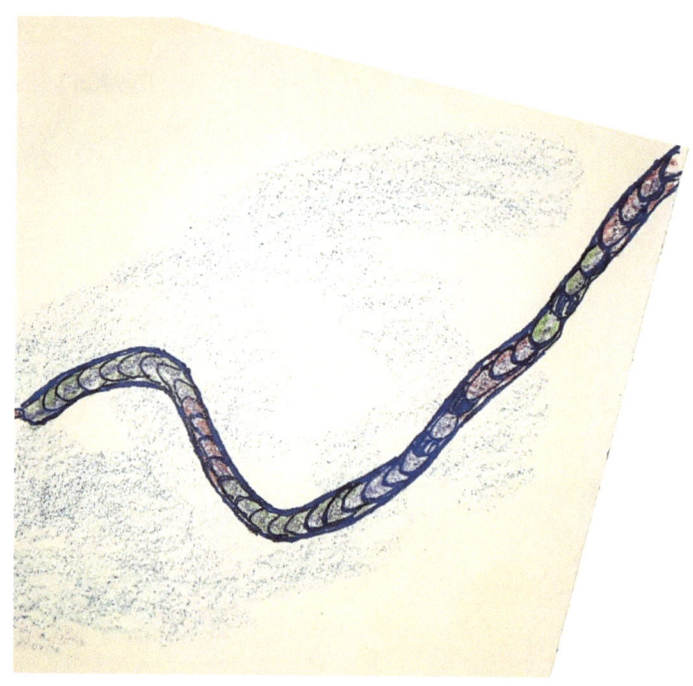

When I was very small,
we sometimes saw
a Great Kite.

> Prompts start here.

> How do you imagine the Great Kite?
>
> Give yourself time to think before you turn the page...

The Great Kite was huge
and provided shade
for people underneath.

How does it feel to find shade on a super hot day?

Picture that feeling.

Draw it here, add some words of your own,
or just hold onto that feeling.

Later, when those same people
   were feeling hot and tired
      or worried by the sun,
they remembered the Great Kite's shade
   and the relief they felt
      and they were extra happy
         for a few moments.

Sometimes,
they remembered
the Great Kite's shade
long enough to work together

to build some shade for each other
and to give everyone a turn
    under the shade they had.

The Great Kite sometimes
gave shelter from the rain
to people underneath.

Plants need water,
and people and other animals need water.

And sometimes rain feels great
-- especially if we're dressed for it.
But sometimes we're just not ready to be soaked.

Remember, or imagine,
a time when you were not ready for rain
and got really, really wet.

How would a Great Kite's floating shelter feel
at a time like that?

Later, when those same people
felt wet
    and cold
        and dripped upon,
they remembered
the Great Kite's shelter
and the comfort they felt,
and they were extra happy
for a few moments.

Sometimes, they remembered
the Great Kite's shelter
long enough to work together
to build rain shelters for each other
and be sure everyone had a turn
under the roofs they had.

Think of a time when rain
or other things around you were difficult.
Write or draw -- or just hold onto
-- some thoughts.

Remember, or try to imagine,
how things could be drier or less difficult.
When things are bad,
does the better picture make you
happier?
sadder?
ready to do something?

Very often,
the Great Kite would be
a special vision
for people who saw it floating by.

How do you think people saw the Great Kite?
Did everyone see the same thing?
Did everyone feel the same when they saw it?
Draw or write your ideas.

Later,
when those same people were feeling
sad,
  or lonely
      or upset,
they would remember
the Great Kite's beauty
  and the soaring feeling
      of watching it float above.

Sometimes,
they remembered
the Great Kite's beauty
long eough
to work together
to create art for each other

and give everyone a turn
enjoying
the art
they had
and time
to make
their own.

It happened, too,

that the Great Kite

would frighten people

when it soared through the sky.

The Great Kite

didn't communicate

   like people do

      or listen

         if they shouted for it

to move away from the fireworks

    or to get out of the way

        when its shadow

            was not what people wanted.

Sometimes people felt
or heard it flapping
like a terrible storm.

It was so large,
and it was not like
other things that people saw.

Later,
when those same people were
    angry or
        unhappy,
they would remember
how the Great Kite scared them
and seemed so strange.

Sometimes,

they would remember those things

long enough that

they found it hard
to settle down together

and even made each other grumpy

... just because.

When things got that way,

it was really hard
for people to remember

the Great Kite's shadow
in the heat

or the Great Kite's shelter
on a rainy day.

They didn't think of its beauty,

    or even of its hugeness --

    just the ways

    that it wasn't exactly

        what they wanted right then.

Thoughts to share?

**Write or draw here
or take time to talk about your ideas.**

One day, I was busy

and all alone.

I felt the Great Kite passing,

and I noticed a funny thing.

  A small flapping inside me,

    like the tiniest of kites.

I imagined I could ride

   and took it for a flight.

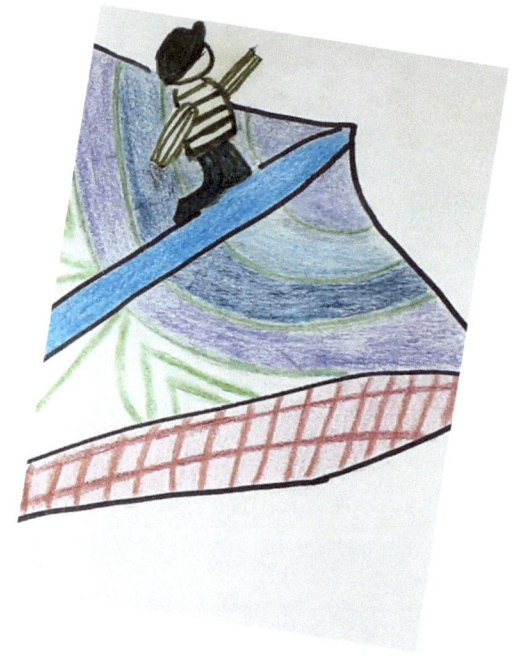

I was part of shadow

      and shelter

      and beauty.

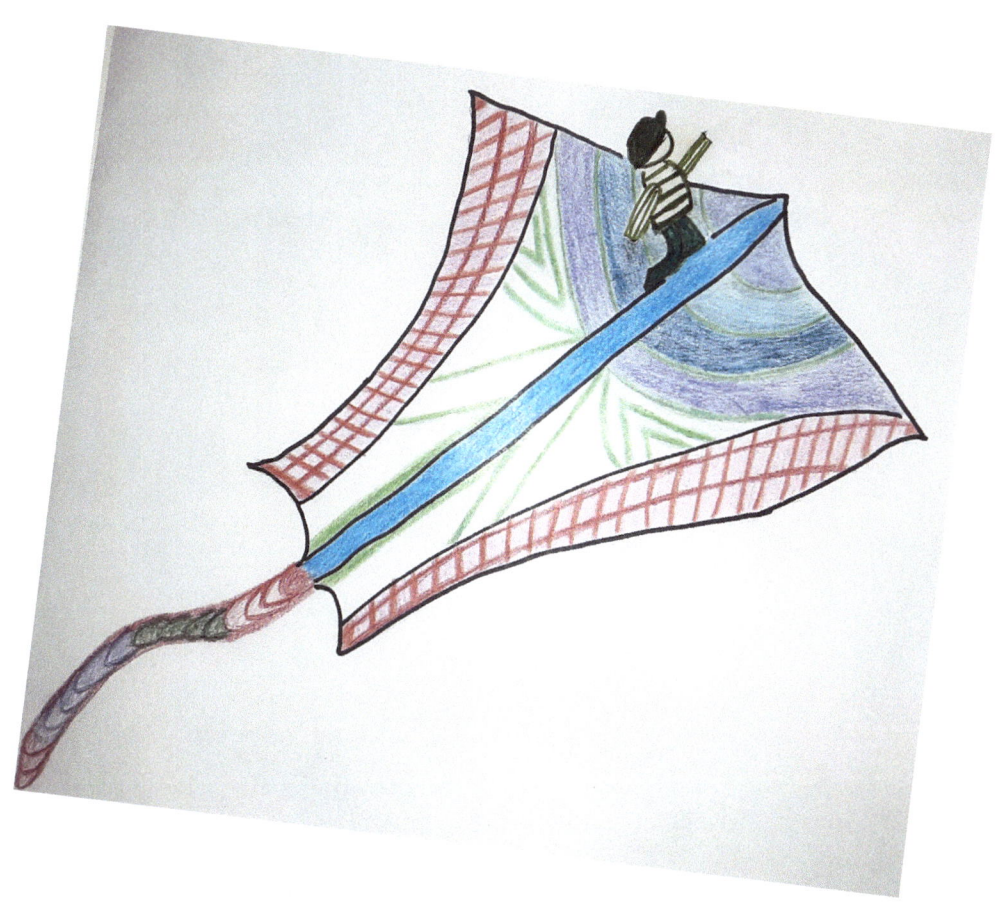

I was strange

   and flapping

      and not exactly

         what people
            around me already knew.

Do people around you expect things
to be one way
most of the time?

What about people?
Do others expect them to be only one way?
Do you?

Do you think
people see
your whole, large
-- and maybe strange -- self?
Sometimes?
Never?
Write or draw some thoughts.
Or just hold onto them.

And then I was just regular,

busy

and all alone.

Until the next time

I felt the tiny kite string pull.

We sometimes saw a Great Kite,
when I was very small.

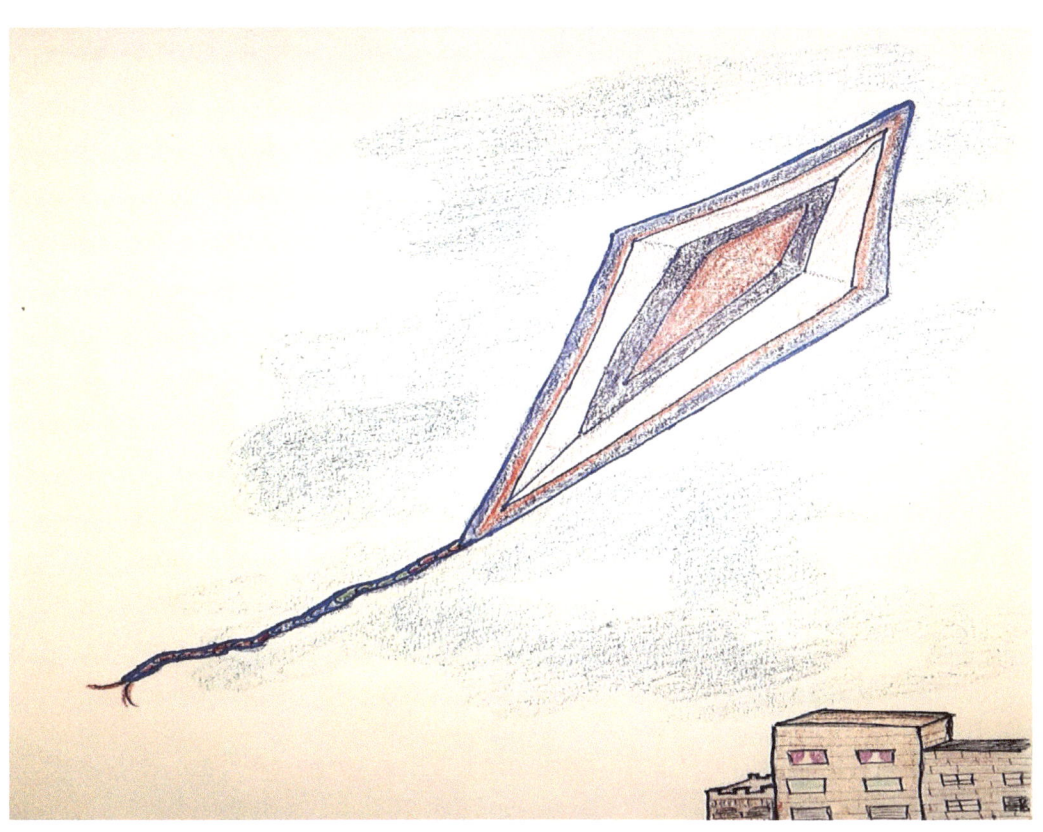

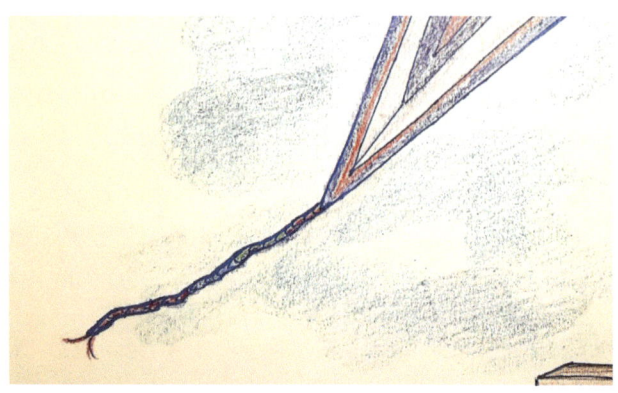

This book is offered by We Act Radio's Charnice Milton Community Bookstore to encourage reading, imagination, and conversation about books and ideas.

We hope that this publication will inspire readers to create and share their own words, artwork, and books!

Instead of professional illustration, this edition includes the author's untrained, raw drawings as part of an encouragement to the reader to fill in their own visions. A new edition, with additional artwork, is planned.

**To share artwork for the new edition
-- work from all ages welcome! --
contact ethreporter@gmail.com.**

Charnice Milton Community Bookstore

Charnice Milton Community Bookstore honors the memory of DC journalist Charnice A. Milton (6/19/87– 5/27/15), shot to death, not far from where the bookstore is now located, on her way home from assignment. The project began at We Act Radio studios in Historic Anacostia. We collect books and donations to support literacy events, providing free books to readers of all ages.

Busboys and Poets-Anacostia, a block away, operates a CMCB branch, offering used books for sale and children's books for free. These operations began on May 27, 2019 with an event honoring Charnice's legacy and dedicating a specially commissioned sculpture, crafted by local artist Mercedes from bullet casings, to her memory.

As we continue to grow, CMCB holds periodic events, on site and around the community, to provide local youth with books to build their home libraries. In addition, we sell adult books locally for nominal fees and are working toward an on-line collection to sell donated adult books at market rate in support of our local literacy efforts. The collaboration with BBP-Anacostia continues to evolve.

www.weluvbooks.org

About the Author

Virginia Avniel Spatz is a freelance writer in Washington, DC, and project manager for CMCB at We Act Radio. She is former feature reporter for We Act Radio's Education Town Hall and serves as webmaster for www.educationtownhall.org.

songeveryday.org --- vspatz.wordpress.com

THANKS

This piece grew from two bits of inspiration:

-- "Opening the Eye of the Heart," a class offered by Baraka Blue's Rumi Center for Spirituality and the Arts, and
-- a very young friend's description of an earthquake as a kite shaking the house.

My four-year-old friend George has been opening the eye of my heart since I first met him at one week of age. Thanks to George for all he taught, and continues to teach, me; to his brother, Francis, for different lessons; and to their parents for sharing these young teachers with me....with another on the way.

Thanks to hip hop artist and mystic poet Baraka Blue; to fellow "Eye of the Heart" students; and to Center DC, an inclusive community based on Islamic values, who introduced me to this teacher.

Thanks also to Maya Gonzalez, ReflectionPress, and School of the Free Mind for some of the ideas behind this book.

Finally, thanks to We Act Radio and Charnice Milton Community Bookstore for fostering community, artistic creation and sharing, cooperative economics, love of books and reading, and the willingness to #dosomething.

-- Virginia, December 2019

RESOURCES:
https://www.rumicenterworkshops.com/
https://www.centerdc.community/
https://reflectionpress.com/

www.ingramcontent.com/pod-product-compliance
Lightning Source LLC
Chambersburg PA
CBHW042127080426
42734CB00001B/25